We Don't Think Racist!

Soothing Affirmations from People of Color

AMANDA MEADOWS & ROBIN HIGGINS

Photos by Aaron Alpert

THE DEVASTATOR

Received On

SEP -- 2016

Magnolia Library

D0707560

WRITTEN BY
AMANDA MEADOWS & ROBIN HIGGINS

PHOTOS BY
AARON ALPERT

DESIGN BY
MIKE REDDY

EDITOR
GEOFFREY GOLDEN

Copyright © 2016 The Devastator, Amanda Meadows, and Robin Higgins.

ALL RIGHTS RESERVED. No part of this parody can be reproduced
or transmitted in any form or by any means
without the permission of the copyright owner.

ISBN-10: 1-942099-07-X

ISBN-13: 978-1-942099-07-9

First Edition: April 2016

devastatorpress.com

PRINTED IN ~~POST-RACIAL AMERICA~~ KOREA

We Don't Think You're Racist! is a work of satire. All names and characters who appear in this parody
are fictional and satirical representations. Any similarities to *We Don't Think You're Racist!*
creations and living persons are purely coincidental. Also, don't sue us. We have no money!

NO LONGER PROPERTY OF
SEATTLE PUBLIC LIBRARY

Dedicated to *reverse racism*.

Dear Caring Ally,

We, the people of color in the world, want to congratulate you on being so open minded. You are perfect.

You understand every single ethnic group without prejudice. You know everything about our food and hairstyles. You are aware of the dances.

When you sing along to our songs, our souls sing with you.

We laud you for your empathy and generosity of spirit to all people of color, collectively and as individuals. It is with gratitude that we pay you this blessing.

You are not racist.

If you fear that the racial bias deeply embedded within our society has tained your worldview, let us put your mind at ease. You are simply far too evolved.

When you utter a word in any other language, we appreciate that you spent your valuable time learning that one word. That one momentous word which closed a gap.

Ally, we made this book for you. Hold it dear to your wise heart.

Read this book the next time a think piece, celebrity tweet, or even a friend makes you feel as if you might have been a little racist. And remember this mantra:

That doesn't apply to me, because I get it.

Fist bump,

All Minorities

You can touch
my hair!
You can
touch my hair
all day.

You know what?

I couldn't
live without
tacos either.

Tell me more
about how
your cousin
teaches
English in Korea.

If I <u>were</u>
a waiter,
I'd love to
refill your glass!

It's a good thing
you "don't see color,"
because I'm
totally blushing.

I <u>do</u> know where to get some super authentic pork adobo.

Let's go right now!

Of course
we can
talk about
Hello Kitty!

You're right.

I get the
best of
both worlds!

You can't be
basic!

You went to
Sarah Lawrence!

¡Omg!

I know it's totally
cray
I don't speak
Spanish!

I'll tell you why
I don't wear a
hijab
if you tell me
where you got
that awesome
necklace!

So Stylish

That's a
cool hat.

Jamaican culture
is fun for
everyone!

My biggest turn-on
is being called spicy.

Good work!

Thanks for only
asking me **twice**
if I'm <u>sure</u>
I'm biracial.

It's true, I am a math expert!

YOU + ME =
A LASTING
FRIENDSHIP
BASED ON MUTUAL
RESPECT

You've dated
three
black guys?

I guess you <u>are</u>
blacker than me!

Sure,
I don't mind detailing
my parents' escape
from Syria,
even at a chill BBQ.

Wow.

"What are you?"

That is a **deep** and existential question.

The keen
pronunciation of
your lunch order
honors
my heritage.

You're right.
Not saying
the **N-word**
<u>does</u> give it
too much power.

Me?
Pass for white?
I'd be honored!

I do
like **soccer!**

What a cool guess
you just made.

Thanks for not automatically assuming my dick is small!

Kudos for waiting
until the <u>end</u> of brunch
to mention the recent
police shooting.

Please don't stop.

I want to hear more
about your
Dominican nanny.

I'm so glad you
informed me
Mulan
is your favorite
Disney Princess.

Sure, I'll fix
your email.
I absolutely love
fixing email!

I'm well-spoken?

Me feel
so gud
rite now.

One tequila

Two tequila

Three tequila

FOUR

...is the number of times you have to assume I'm a valet before I'm offended.

So you still have 2 left!

You're only attracted to Asian women?

Cooooooool.

If I'm "one of the
good ones,"
then you're clearly
the best
of the best!

That's fair to ask.

I <u>am</u> like
a human GPS
for Mecca.

MECCA

I guess if I
time traveled,
I __would__
have to be a slave.

Way to keep
those hypotheticals
realistic!

If I asked you
not to do that
funny accent,
I'd be taking away
<u>your</u> freedom.

My "Indian name" is
Impressed
By Your Smart
Questions.

I'd **love**
to see your
Mohammed
cartoon!

Everyday, I wonder:

Why isn't there affirmative action for really down white dudes?

Hey, I could tell you almost crossed the street to avoid me, but ultimately didn't.

I'd like to hereby present you this medal for "Excellence in Being Not Racist."

ACTOR CREDITS

in order of appearance

 Aliza Pearl is an actor, writer, improviser, and producer of diverse sci-fi. She performs full-length improvised genre plays at Impro Studio. Always busy, but always makes time to tweet NASA regularly. Website: alizapearl.com

 Paul Heredia is a comedian and writer for Fruit Chicken Comedy. He performs, writes, and hosts shows at iO West and Second City Hollywood. Website: fruitchicken.com

 Minhdzuy Khorami is a comedian and actor who can be found singing nerdy songs in his musical comedy duo, Mudville Comedy. He has tricked a good amount of his friends into thinking he works at Pixar. Website: minhdzuyinhd.com

 Aaron Covington is a writer and comedian in Los Angeles who co-wrote the critically acclaimed 2015 film Creed. Twitter: @bearcov

 Raiza Licea is an actor and comedian born and raised in Miami. You can see her performing with her favorite UCB improv teams Bruce or Willis, Geraldo, Improvisos Peligrosos, and Romper Farts. Twitter: @raizalicea

 Joaquin Poblete is a Los Angeles based producer and director who specializes in music videos, tour videography and digital content. Website: vimeo.com/joaquinpoblete

 Ann Maddox has been performing at UCB Theatre LA since 2005. She has written for NPR, and appeared on Two Broke Girls, The Office, and Grandfathered. Twitter: @Mikiannmaddox

 Joe Cabello is a writer and comedian in Los Angeles. Find his humor books The Longest Haiku and The Farts Awakens: A Star Wars Parody on Amazon. Twitter: @joecabello

 Lorraine DeGraffenreidt performs improv, sketch and stand up comedy in Los Angeles. She also produces live events for the UCB Touring Company. Twitter: @lorrrrraine

 Matt Apodaca is a writer and comedian in Los Angeles who manages UCB LA. He has two cats that he's only mildly allergic to. Twitter: @mattapodaca

 Vida Ghaffari is an award-winning actress and voiceover artist who has performed sketch and improv at UCB, iO West and Second City. She also blogs about fashion and beauty at soveryvida.com. Twitter: @vidaghaffari

Oscar Montoya is a comedian, dancer, and writer who works as a director for the arts education company Story Pirates. He can be seen in his house sketch team Sidekick at iO West and Harold improv team Nomi Malone at UCB LA. Twitter: @ozzymo

 Carla Valderrama is an actress, comedian, and ghetto super star who performs at UCB Theatre. Follow your heart and her Instagram: @profaneangel

 Robin Higgins is a comedy writer and performer who co-authored this book. Higgins co-founded humor site The Higgs-Weldon and is a member of UCB Mess Hall team The Up and Up. Website: thehiggsweldon.com.

 Elan' Trinidad is an Eisner Award Nominated cartoonist. He has also worked on animated shows like The Simpsons, Miles From Tomorrowland, and Sheriff Callie's Wild West. Twitter: @T_of_E_comics

 Danielle Radford is a comedian and writer who has performed on Flophouse on Viceland, as well as at clubs, colleges and festivals across the country. Website: danielle-radford.com

 Maddox is a genius and thought leader behind the The Best Page in the Universe. Don't go to his website. Twitter: @maddoxrules

 Zan Poka is an actor and photographer in Los Angeles. Follow her on Twitter: @zandorasbox

Ewan Chung is an actor, singer, producer, writer, and polyglot. Evidence of his work can be found at vimeo.com/ewanchung. Twitter: @ewanchung

Lonnie Millsap is a single panel cartoonist whose work can be found on Amazon and in Barnes & Noble. Millsap releases his sixth book of humorous cartoons in spring 2016. Website: lonniemillsap.com

 Lars Ingelman is inventor of the reverse telephone and an animation professional, whose credits include *Moonbeam City* and the upcoming feature *Nerdland*. Twitter: @CartoonLars

 Jessica Keenan is a stand-up comedian in Los Angeles. Twitter: @jlkeenancomedy

 Tadamori Yagi is an actor who has been in numerous commercials and TV shows, including *Southland* and *Parenthood*. He performs at the Catsby comedy show at The Clubhouse Comedy Club in Los Angeles. Website: tadamoriyagi.com

 Chanel Horn is a college student majoring in Business Marketing and plans for a career in Public Relations.

 Renie Rivas is an actor, comedian, and improviser in Los Angeles whose credits include the film *DisOrientation* and various TV commercials. She graduated the Upright Citizens Brigade Training Center and wrote for cult satirical anthology series *The Devastator*. Twitter: @Renie_Rivas

 Lesley Tsina is a writer and actor who has appeared on *Conan*, *Black-ish*, *Community* and is the author of *Restart Me Up: The Unauthorized, Un-Accurate Oral History of Windows 95*. Website: lesleytsina.com

 Raj Desai has performed stand-up on *The Late Late Show*, and has written for Comedy Central, The Higgs Weldon and more. Twitter: @_rajdesai

 Amanda Meadows is a comedy writer who co-authored this book. She has written for McSweeney's, Jim Henson Company, *Paste Magazine*, and is co-publisher of The Devastator, the only all comedy press in America. Website: devastatorpress.com

 Aristotle C. Acevedo is a podcast producer for Nerdist and runs ZineMelt at Meltdown Comics. Twitter: @aristacos

 Connie Shin is a comedian and writer who currently writes sketches for UCB LA Maude. She also performs in her indie sketch team Basic Bitches. Twitter: @Thatconnieshin

 Alex Cottrell is an actor in LA. You might find him in commercials or various web content. Instagram: @Alex__Cottrell

 Ruha Taslimi is an artist who can be seen performing with her UCB LA Mess Hall team Moon Hundred, her musical improv team Sing! Sing!, and in the Story Pirates. Twitter: @Ruhahaha

 Hayley Marie Norman is an actor, producer, and writer who regularly appears in your favorite TV shows and movies! See her on TRU TV's *Adam Ruins Everything* or performing in UCB LA digital team Sancho. Twitter: @xohayleymarie

 Nik Dodani is an actor, comedian, and activist whose latest happenings can be found on nikdodani.com/shamefulplugs. Twitter: @nikdodani

 Joey Clift is a comedy writer who has written both Bugs Bunny cartoons for Warner Brothers and song parodies listed on Rap Genius. He is currently senior staff writer for comedy website Sarcasm Society and a member of sketch comedy trio Local Business Comedy. Twitter: @joeytainment

 Mal Merpi is a comedian and writer who runs the popular blog Tinder No Filter (@tindernofilter). When she's not slaying punks on Tinder, she's rolling cats on the Fox lot, or performing on stage at UCB LA. Twitter: @purpledmal

 Asterios Kokkinos is a writer and comedian *oh god you've stopped reading this haven't you?* Follow him on Twitter @asterios if that last thing made you laugh. Website: asterioskokkinos.com

 Zora Bikangaga is a writer, actor, and creator of independent comedy series, *The HOA*. He also performs with freestyle rap improv group 8C8 Hip-Hop Improv. Twitter: @ZoraBikangaga

 Genetra Tull is a comedian and writer who performs with her sketch team This is Not a Tan and UCB Mess Hall team Fresh Kicks. Website: genetratull.com

Thank you to everyone involved
in putting this book together!
We couldn't have pulled this off without the
hilarious and generous LA comedy community.

THANKS TO THE DEVASTATOR AUTHOR CORPS:
Patrick Baker, Joan Ford, Asterios Kokkinos,
Lesley Tsina, Lynne Donahue, Micki Grover, Lee Keeler,
Kenny Keil, Paige Weldon, Joe Starr, Ryan Sandoval;
and this book's editor, Geoffrey Golden.

THANKS TO THESE FUNNY AND SUPPORTIVE PEOPLE:
Joey Clift, Raj Desai, Connie Shin, Shing Yin Khor, Taneka Neeks,
Isabel Higgins, Holly Golden, Chanel Horn, and Hassan Hahim.

ROBIN HERE!
Thanks to my parents, Sharon and George Higgins for teaching me
how to work hard and care about issues like this,
and also for raising me in Oakland, CA, the best city ever.

AMANDA HERE!
Thanks to my mom, Rajae, who came from Morocco and
bravely endured Islamophobia in the 80s, 90s, 00s,
and today. Thanks to my dad, Raymond,
for showing me at a young age what it means
to be a black man in America.

YOU MIGHT ALSO LIKE THESE DEVASTATOR PRESS JOINTS:

STAY-AT-HOME SCARFACE
A coloring and activity book for dope new dads.

KILLING IT
The action girl's guide to saving the world (while looking hot).

THE
DEVASTATOR
MAKES FUNNY BOOKS
It's what we do, you guys!

ALL THE FEELINGS
A master class for tween actors, with monologues for *every* emotion.

THE PRESIDENTIAL DICKERBOOK
Put a penis sticker on every POTUS.

DEVASTATORPRESS.COM

A racist person
would never read
this book.